At this time, the Philistines were enemies of the Israelites. The two armies faced each other across a valley, ready for battle. David's three oldest brothers had joined the Israelite army to fight.

One day, David's father Jesse asked him to take food to his brothers at the battlefield. "Take this grain and these loaves of bread to your brothers," said Jesse, "and bring back news of how they are doing."

Goliath was over nine feet tall. He wore a heavy coat of bronze armor and carried a spear with a tip as heavy as a bowling ball. Every day for forty days, he had challenged the Israelites to send someone to fight him.

"This story reminds every child that no matter how small they are, with faith in God and courage in their hearts, they can face any giant and win."

(And remember, with God, All Things Are Possible!)

Thank you for reading David and Goliath!
If you and your child enjoyed this story, please consider leaving a review—it helps others discover the book too!
✺ Your feedback means the world!
👉 And if you haven't already, grab your own copy today to enjoy this inspiring Bible story again and again!

THE END

Printed in Dunstable, United Kingdom